Seven Secrets
to Success

SELF
PUBLISHER
GUIDE

SAMUEL WARDWELL & RODNEY BELL

REBELL BOOKS

Atlanta, Georgia

www.RebellBooks.com

ISBN: 978-1-953282-04-0

Nonfiction > Language Arts & Disciplines > Authorship
Nonfiction > Language Arts & Disciplines > Publishing

REBELL BOOKS
Atlanta Georgia

Printed in the United States

Acknowledgements

I would like to sincerely thank Samuel Wardwell for his partnership and expertise; Thomas Blackburn for his diligence in this project. I also want to acknowledge my 'not so secret' weapons, Magnus, Jonas, Jordan, Joshua, Justin and Matthew. I especially want to acknowledge my forever go to person and inspiration Evette Collier-Bell, my rock.

Rodney Bell

I would like to thank my partner, Rodney Bell, for all of the behind the scenes work that has made our publishing and marketing company such a great success. Also, much thanks and love for my wife, Kathy. She is my greatest supporter and cheerleader. To our team and support staff that help our authors find success, thanks, guys. We would not be able to make such a difference in the publishing world without you.

Samuel Wardwell

Dedicated

To all who take pen in hand and
capture their thoughts.

Preface

You're a good writer, but even if you were not your books should still sell. To prove a point; Ever bought a book you did not like? Of course, you have. So, have most readers.

Readers bought their book because of its packaging and they will buy yours too... If it is packaged right!

We whole heartedly believe that good books will sell!

But to do so, you must publish your book right.

To be successful, the book must meet industry-accepted Publishing and Marketing standards.

But that is just the beginning.

When you decide to self-publish a book, you are signing up for all the duties a traditional publisher would typically do for you. This means you not only have to write a great book, but you also take on the responsibilities of publishing and marketing it.

There are 7 Key Factors essential to enjoying great book sales. We have detailed all of them here.

Self-publishing does not have to be complicated, but it also cannot be taken lightly. For self-published authors, there are many book marketing strategies and tactics that can be employed. While some may seem quite direct or even relatively "simple," it is quite easy to make mistakes that can derail a book.

The world of publishing comes with some degrees of disappointments, but it also comes with many rewards. Use this guide to minimize the setbacks and maximize the rewards.

R.E. Bell

Table of Contens

Advice to Self-Publisher

Not to give anything away, but in reality, there are no "hidden secrets" to being a bestseller. If there is any secret at all, it is finding somebody who understands what is necessary to package your book for the public and who is familiar with what it takes to market your book in this evolving industry.

Here lays the challenge. How do you know if your publisher really understands what it takes to market your book? We will explain to you the *seven primary factors* needed to make your book a bestseller.

The problem authors have today is finding a publisher who understands that the "old school" way of doing things does not work anymore. Almost without exception, new authors end up rejected time and time again by traditional publishing companies who would not have a clue how to market your book in the first place. Even the so-called self-publishing companies rarely do anything to market your work. They tend **not** to be much more than editing and printing businesses.

So, what should a new author do?

First, you must admit to yourself that, most likely, you are an unknown author with an untested commodity (your book) in an industry that produces about 3000 new books every day. If you are not either famous or, for that matter, infamous, then a traditional publisher is not going to give you the time of day. So, what do you do? If you want your book published, then you have to go the self-publishing route. And by the way, we show you why the **right** self-publishing company can be the best way to go.

Second, you must understand what questions must be answered before you move ahead with a self-publishing company. To start with, most of them are not in business to *market* your books. In fact, they usually have no clue *how* to get your books in front of the reading public. You typically end up with hundreds-of-copies of books that might as well be used to decorate the walls of your family room. How does the average self-publishing company make its money? They do it by charging you exorbitant fees to *supposedly* edit your work, format your book for printing, creating a questionable cover that might not live up to industry standards, and then convincing you to purchase a thousand copies to get their best discount rate.

Now, what do you do? Ask yourself this... Do you know **what questions to ask** before you get started? Do you know how to **avoid being misled** by dreams of bestseller status with no explanation explaining how to market your book?

The following information in "*7 Secrets of the Bestseller*" will discuss just what you have to do to make your book a great success. It's not a difficult concept. The real secret is understanding what questions you need to ask not only your publisher-to-be but to **ask yourself** as an author wanting to have a best-selling book.

But before you turn the page. You must decide if you *really* want to be a best-selling author. It takes work, commitment to your goals, and the willingness to do what is necessary to become a success. If you believe in yourself and want to get started, then please let us introduce to you what you need to do to become a bestselling author.

Samuel Wardwell

Introduction

Secrets of the Bestseller

Congratulations! You have taken on the challenge of becoming a bestselling author.

Whether you are a new author looking to get your work to the reading public or are frustrated with your current publisher because of poor sales, we can help you become a bestseller.

As we mentioned before, there really are no hidden secrets. The challenge for authors is not having a clue where to start. To make matters even more difficult, almost all publishing companies either do not understand today's competitive bookselling market or refuse to adjust to the changing times.

As an up and coming author, you must first understand that for all intents and purposes, you are starting your own business. This is especially true if you choose the self-publishing route. With this in mind, you cannot assume that your publisher-to-be is anything other than a vendor looking to make a profit off of your work. Of course, publishing companies are looking for clients to partner with for the long haul. However, you cannot assume that they are always looking out for your best interests.

Most authors start out trying to solicit traditional publishing companies in hopes of receiving some kind of fee for their work. The odds of a new author, who is not already famous or directly associated with a huge database of potential book-buyers, receiving a contract for their work is less than 1 in a 100. The same result is typical when trying to find a literary agent to handle your book. So most of the new authors brought to print end up choosing the self-publishing company route.

Picking the right self-publishing company requires understanding what is necessary to get your book to market. The first thing you have to understand is that as soon as you choose to go the self-publishing route, you are choosing to start your own business. You must prepare yourself by understanding the seven key-factors necessary for success. You also must understand that your success will depend on how much effort you are willing to put into the marketing of your work.

Let's talk a little about what most self-publishing companies do for you.

When you review the services supplied by self-publishing companies, they typically include taking your manuscript from words and pictures in a computer-file and turning it into a real-life book that can be held in your hands and enjoyed. They also offer services like setting up a website, social media pages, and handling the distribution of your book. Once your book is published, they then offer you a price list that shows you how you can supposedly make more money by printing 100s of copies of your work.

This is all great stuff, right? You now have your book and a pallet of additional copies sitting in a warehouse. But do you know what you don't have? You do not have a marketing plan!

How are readers going to know about your book? Even more important of a concern, why should people care about your book? As an author, who are you, and why did you write the book in the first place?

This is what most publishers leave out. Their goal is to do a great job creating a book for you and developing all of the tools you need, but they do not show you how to use the tools and the pitfalls of distributing your work with no marketing plan.

The first thing you must learn is that *you* are the most important element in the marketing of your work. Who are you? Why should I care about you? Why did you write your book? Why should I read your book? Most self-publishing companies really do not care about any of these questions.

What they care about is printing and selling you lots of copies of your work.

So, let's talk about the steps necessary for you to succeed in the publishing world. The four questions asked in the previous paragraph must be answered by you before you get started. If you already have published your book and have been unsuccessful selling more than a few copies, then its never too late to rethink what you need to do to relaunch your work.

In our modern world, you must understand that almost all books are purchased online. And the dominant online behemoth that monopolizes the industry is Amazon.com. So, if books are mostly purchased online, it is important to realize that you must have an online presence, too. If you haven't already developed an author website and a social media base, you must start working on this immediately.

Let the world know who you are and what you enjoy. Start to interact with like-minded individuals who might become readers of your work. The more you work on your online profile, the more people out there who will eventually be interested in your work.

The good news is that it is never too late to take advantage of our "7 *Secrets of the Bestseller*." The challenge is finding the right publisher, who is not just an overblown printing company. We are going to give you the ammunition needed to not only make the right choice but also to allow you to feel comfortable in the knowledge that you now understand the process.

Let's take a look at the seven key factors you should keep in the back of your mind as you travel the road from *author-with-a-manuscript* to bestseller.

THE 7 SECRETS

Secret #1
Cover Design

General Rule: No more than 2 primary colors. Only one scene. Colors must match genre. Font must match Genre. No wordiness or clutter.

What is the first thing that a potential reader sees when they are shopping for their next book? The answer is the book cover, of course. Now, what is the next thing a potential buyer does after they look at the front cover? They flip the book over to look at the back cover. This is true whether the reader is looking at a physical book or perusing your work online.

So, what is the big secret of cover design? After all, it should have your name on it, the title of the book, and a *pretty* picture that reflects what the book is all about... Right?

Well, no. A book cover needs a lot more than that. The cover must draw the reader to what's inside. But even more important than drawing the reader's eye, it must also supply Internet search engines with the factors needed to find your book in the first place.

The cover design is not just a graphic arts project. Every genre has its own color scheme. This is true whether you are writing a romance novel or creating a how-to book to explain bridge construction -- Colors and cover layouts change with the subject of the book. There is an art to understanding this and the psychology that determines what the reader's mind is looking for.

Simple things like the placement of the title versus the location of the author's name are important. A well-known author's name is usually on top of the front cover, while an unknown author should have the title of the book prominently displayed.

Always be careful about making a cover too busy. Having too many people prominently displayed on your cover can make it seem overwhelming and can unconsciously confuse a potential reader. Your cover should display an event or specific thought, rather than trying to describe everything happening in your book.

When discussing your cover design with your publisher, it is very important that you have a lot of input. However, it is also important that you listen to your designer's reasons for their layout and color choices. What looks great to you might be confusing or distracting to a potential buyer. This is extremely important when you are writing a work of fiction. Fictional novels are more difficult to market because there are so many of them out there. Making your book stand out above the crowd can help your sales, especially at book fairs and shows.

But don't forget the spine and back cover work. The front cover attracts the reader. The back cover explains to the reader what is inside and why they should want to read what you have to say.

The two primary things on the back cover are your author's bio and a brief but motivating description of your work. This description is extremely important when trying to sell a fictional work to a reader.

Having an author's picture is also important. Readers want to get to know the author. Just make sure that your picture is professionally done and a headshot. You want to do the best you can to look the part of an author-in-the-know about their work.

Another consideration that can be extremely important when your readers are searching for your work is a *subtitle*.

Subtitles may not seem important, but there are literally millions of books out there. You want to do everything you can to make your work stand out above the competition. Plus, your subtitle will assist those pesky Internet search engines with finding your book in the first place.

Here are two examples of covers for the same book.

The first cover had all the right colors and looked good, but it had no subtitle. The second cover had what turns out to be the all-important subtitle. By itself, the subtitle dramatically increased the number of successful hits by readers searching for their next read. Plus, by slightly offsetting the colors in the title and subtitle, the reader's eye was drawn down the page. This was important when trying to get the reader to turn the book over to see the info on the back.

Same book, but much better results with just a slight modification in the cover design.

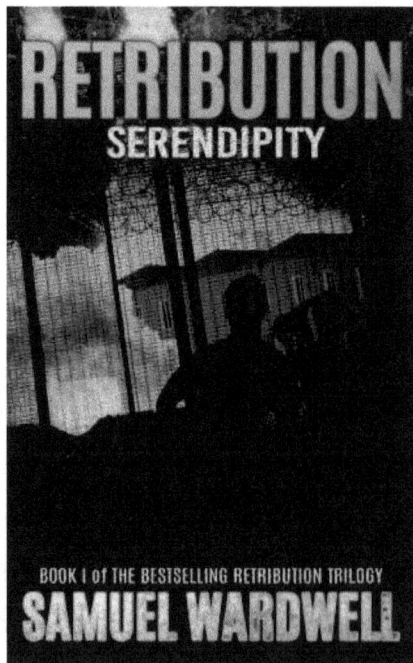

Try it. Google the word "Retribution," then try doing the same thing with "Retribution, Serendipity." The results are dramatic, and the second option takes a reader directly to the author's website and Amazon's sales page.

What is important to remember here is to not only know what you want to see on your cover but also to be willing to understand what is necessary to make your cover and title a successful draw for potential readers.

Secret #2
Title, Subtitle & Short Description

General Rule: Abstract titles are easier to find but more difficult to market. The subtitle should contain a keyword. The short description should be brief, contain several keywords and invite reader to find an answer within book. No info on author.

Your book title and book description are second only in importance to your book cover's image. Amazingly enough, very few publishers understand the importance of both.

Before you can give an adequate description of your book, you need to think-out your title. Don't make the mistake of choosing a title that "feels good." Think about your audience, your book's genre, and what the reading public might be searching for when looking for their next read.

Take this book as an example. The title is "*7 Secrets of the Bestseller, An Authors Self Publisher Guide.*" Now, think about where most books are searched for and purchased. In most cases, the search is done on Google, and the purchase is made on Amazon. For better or worse, in this current and foreseeable market, this is where most readers end up going to find your book.

When surveyed, searches made for books rarely used a book's complete title. Searches typically included words that directly impacted the reader's inquiry. So, if you are writing a how-to book, you want to make sure that in your title or subtitle that you include as many keywords that your potential reader might use in their quest to find their next read.

In the case of this book, take a look at our word choice. "Bestseller," "Author," "Guide," "Self-publisher," "Publisher," and "Secrets" are all used when a writer is looking to publish their work. Remember, search engines take the first part of a word search and autofill for you. Thus, for example, when the word *publish* is entered, the words published, publisher, publishing, etc. will all pop up. This is why subtitles are so very important.

Once you have chosen your book's title, you now want to create a *Book Title & Description* that can be used on Amazon and other venues. This description should be jam-packed with the keywords that a reader's search will discover. By doing this correctly, your book will stand out above the crown and make it easier for retailers, like Amazon, to find.

When looking for a publisher, you need to ask if they understand the importance of this marketing concept. It is easier to create a title and subtitle for non-fiction work. But the same concept is as important for a work of fiction. A good book title and book description have proven to be an inexpensive but extremely effective marketing tool. They dramatically impact your book's ranking and search position.

It's the little things that can make such a huge difference in the marketing of your book.

Always take the time to take into consideration what makes it easier for your readers to find you. After all, you spent hours and hours writing your book. The simple concept of correctly titling and describing your work won't take much longer. And... It is definitely worth the great results.

Secret #3
Genre & Categories

General Rule: Categories of books include New Adult, Young Adult, Novels, and Nonfiction, because they don't communicate anything about the book's content other than whether it's true or not, and sometimes the age range it's meant for.

Genres of books say something about what the book is about. Sci-fi/fantasy, romance, memoir, biography, history, and mysteries are all designations that tell you on a basic level what a book is about.

First, let's talk about what is meant by *genre*.

Since most of us do not go to school to study English History, you are probably not familiar with the five genres of literature. They are Poetry, Drama, Prose, Nonfiction, and Media. Anything you write typically falls into one of these categories. However, each of these genres have subgroups that are far more important for the successful marketing of your book.

In the publishing world, the word *genre* has been expanded to include almost any topic an author chooses to turn into a book. The most common genres in order of popularity are:

1.   Romance/Erotica

2. Crime/Mystery
3. Religious/Inspirational
4. Science Fiction/Fantasy
5. Horror

For better or worse, this is what the reading public is buying, at least as far as Amazon's 2019 sales report. And *Romance/Erotica* has almost as many sales as the next four categories combined.

You want to choose a genre that adequately reflects the subject of your work. Today, publishers only use four genres of books. They are New Adult, Young Adult, Novels, and Nonfiction. Subcategories, like Sci-fi/fantasy, romance, memoir, biography, history, mysteries, how-to books, etc. are all designations that tell on a basic level what a book is about. These subcategories all help focus your potential reader's search toward your book.

So, what does this mean for you as an author trying to choose your book's genre?

No, you should not place your "How to install a Dishwasher" book under *Crime/Mystery* in the hope of getting more sales. Although I sometimes think it should be a *crime* to force us to use the horrible directions usually included with your purchase. Thank goodness for YouTube. But, I am getting off-topic here. What you do need to do is to learn how to niche your book under an appropriate genre, then choose subcategories that are commonly used by Amazon and other book retailers.

By picking the right genre and subcategories, you will be amazed at how easy it can be to become a bestseller in your book's category.

Earlier, we talked about the experience Samuel Wardwell had when his first novel was released. His publisher did not prepare him adequately for the modern marketing world. The original subcategory for his novel, "Retribution," was *Action/Adventure*. If you review Amazon's top five categories for best sales, you'll immediately notice that the words *action* and *adventure* are not mentioned. When the book was re-released using the improved subcategory placement techniques, the updated book was renamed "Retribution, Serendipity," and placed as a *crime* novel with a touch of *romance*. By adding a subtitle and changing the subcategory choices, the same book with an updated title and genre placement took off like a rocket heading toward the moon.

The lesson here is to make sure that your publisher understands the importance of book titles and subtitles, genre placement, and choosing the best subcategories for your work. Done correctly, you'll be leaps and bounds ahead of your competition.

Secret #4
Keyword Optimization

General Rule: Include some keywords in Book Description and Author Bio. Choose keywords that are highly searched to find other successful books that are similar to yours

We talked a little bit about keywords when choosing your title. They are also important to use when writing your book's description, both for Amazon and for the back cover of your book.

Let us have some fun and go back to an earlier title, "How to Install a Dishwasher." If you were writing a how-to book about this subject, you would want to make sure that it was easy for a potential reader to find. So, let's see if you have learned anything about titles and subtitles.

First, when choosing the title of your book, you always want it to reflect what your book is about. In this case, our topic is a dishwasher and how to install it. But is the title enough as it stands? Think about this. It costs you nothing to add a subtitle that will add additional words describing your book. Let's see... What if we created a subtitle like: A Handy Instruction Guide.

Now, look at what you have accomplished. Between your title and subtitle, you have the following keywords you can use to assist retailers, like Amazon, and search engines, like Google, with finding your book. Here's what you could choose for your keywords:

Handy (Handyman)
Install (Installation)
Dish (Dishwasher)
Handy (Handyman, Handywoman, etc.)
Instruct (Instruction, Instructions,
Guid (Guide, Guidance)

Typically, Amazon searches allow for seven keywords. If you can include several of the keywords in your title, you are way ahead of other books on the same subject. When Amazon does searches, they do not just stop at your title. The keywords are also searched for in your book's description, too.

Remember, Internet searches are not limited only to actual words in the English language. A great example of this is "Guid." It is not a word. But when searched for, it will be autocorrected and filled with options like *guide* and *guidance*.

Although all publishers will ask you for keywords to use for your book, most of them will not assist you with your word choice. This is because most publishers do not have the expertise or understanding of how important the selection of keywords is to the marketing of your work. Make sure that keyword selection is service offered by your publisher. Chosen properly, they will make a huge difference in the number of readers being able to find your book during a search.

Secret #5
Book Reader Reviews

General Rule: Organic reviews boost your books visibility and increases sales. Third party endorsements and recommendations from notable sources increase books perceived value and authors credibility.

There's nothing better than having a review from a real reader not associated with you in any way. This is especially true if the reviewer thinks your work is the greatest book ever written in the history of the world. Well, most of us would be happy if we got four out of five stars. But who's counting anyway?

Seriously though, Book Reader Reviews are extremely important when it comes to the marketing of your book. If a person looking for an appliance goes to the trouble of reading reviews before purchasing, we can promise you that someone looking over your book is going to read your book's reviews, too.

But where do you get reviews? After all, your book has just hit the market. I know, let's have your mother, your spouse, and your four-year-old all write raving reviews! The challenge with doing this is that it usually is obvious when a reviewer has not read your work. Glowing thoughts with no insight into the actual content of the book can turn people off rather than excite them to make the purchase.

This is where a good publisher comes in to help out. Before a book is released to the public, it is a good idea to have one of the hundreds of book-clubs out there take a look at your work first. The problem for new authors is having no access to the appropriate club. A good publisher should be able to assist you with this.

Unless you have written a Tom Clancy sized novel with 15,000 pages of work, it is usually pretty easy to find people to review your book. There are book clubs interested in every genre and topic. Even long fiction novels have a segment of readers looking forward to reviewing your work.

But even if you do not have access to book clubs, it is important that you find at least three people to read and give you a review. In fact, not having any reviews can be worse than having negative reviews. This is because it is better to have at least somebody reading your work than no one interested at all.

Book reviews are considered more important and authentic than endorsements. They have a certain personal feel to them. The other major consideration is that online retail bookstores, including Amazon, exhibit and highlight reviews as part of the book and author pages to help encourage book sales.

Endorsements can help. But anybody looking at them assumes that endorsers are solicited and compensated. So, always go out of your way to have your book reviews lined up. They can make a huge difference.

Secret #6
Biography & Author Page

General Rule: Tell reader why your unique experience gives you a personal and interesting story telling perspective. Leave out the grandchildren.

All book publishers ask for an author's bio. But very few actually sit down and assist you with this important sales tool.

Not only is it useful to know what you need to include in an author's bio, but it is also helpful to know how your vital information should look. Even though very few publishing guides note it, the "Author Bio" section will impact sales and often determine what media you receive.

Remember, odds are you are not already famous. The only way you are going to become well known is to start with a good, concise description of who you are. The author bio, accompanied by a professional-looking portrait picture, allows the reader to learn who you are.

This is especially important if you are writing a non-fiction work that takes some expertise. For example, as the author of "How to Install a Dishwasher, A *Handy Instruction Guide*," you would want to include in your author's bio. It would help the reader know that you have installed hundreds of dishwashers and, in fact, invented the thing in the first place. This would give you more credibility and enhance sales.

If you are writing a fictional work, then it helps to make your background and experiences *real* for the reader. Your publisher should know how to create an appropriate synopsis of who you are that is relatable to your reader.

Visit a bookstore near you. If you cannot find one, then go to your favorite online bookstore. Take a few minutes to read author bios in your book's genre. The fastest way to learn what to do is to review what has worked in the past.

Next, take some time to create a more extensive author's bio for the Author Page on

Amazon. The online titan provides a handy place for customers to learn about you. The Author Page on Amazon also gives you a great place to showplace your work, especially if you have more than one book available.

When a potential reader of your book does an online search, many times they are searching for you, the author, rather than your book title. Unless you are named John Smith, any search should bring up your author's page on Amazon. Oh, and if your name is John Smith, it would help if you added a middle initial or to use a pen name. Many people would be very surprised to learn how many authors do not write under their own names.

Whether you use a pen name or your real name, make sure you spend some time working on your Amazon Author Page. It will help introduce the reading public to you and better educate them about you and your books. The page can display detailed info about your books and can include the links to your website, blogs, and social media posts.

Secret #7
Author Website and Social Media

General Rule: Use your website as a hub to connect all sources i.e. Social Media, Amazon, Goodreads, Podcast, Blog, Store, etc.

An author website can serve as a dynamic tool to promote yourself, your books, and anything else related to your personal brand. It can be used as a central hub to market your book as well as open a beneficial communication channel between you and your fans.

It is crucial that you have your website created professionally. In just the last year alone, many changes have been made to the industry that hosts websites that the general public is only now learning.

One of these changes is the SSL certification. The SSL was created by companies, like GoDaddy, to help eliminate rogue websites with malicious intent and to force sites no longer operated by their original creators to be dissolved. Without the SSL certification, when your site is visited, no virus protection software will allow the visitor to enter the site because it is not secured. Little things like having an unsecured website can deter visitors from entering.

Once you have your website created and set up properly, you want to make it becomes the hub of your *personal brand*.

Today, everything needs to be branded. This means that you want to create a logo, picture, banner, and possibly a trademark that is uniquely yours. Then, you want all of your social media and marketing sites, like Amazon, to be linked in-and-out of your website directly.

Good website management gives you the ability to *capture* your reader's contact info, like their email address, and can direct your viewers to your social media, blogs, and any podcasts you favor. Everything you do should be routed through your website.

As far as the layout of the website goes, simple is best.

Do not go overboard with all kinds of flashy pictures and links to additional pages. This can confuse and frustrate potential readers of your work. Your website should be a landing-pad for readers to be able to learn about you, the author, and your books. Spend your time working on your own branding with a great banner, bio, and links to your books, social media, blogs, and podcasts.

Earlier, we talked a little about the importance of social media. It is never too early to start developing your Internet presence.

We all know that today 99% of all public figures have a strong social media profile and following. If you still can, get your Facebook, Twitter, Instagram, Goodreads, and Linkedin profiles and pages up and running as you write your book. If you have a podcast, make sure that you have links to YouTube, too. If your work has already been released and you have no social media set up for you as an author, then you should immediately get started. At least get your author's Facebook page up, then add the other sites as soon as you possibly can.

If you do not have a social media presence or understand how to use it successfully, it is important that you find an expert to assist you. Typically, social media management consultants are not that expensive, as compared to other publishing costs, and can make a huge difference in your sales.

Of all the social media sites, the most important and most visited is Facebook. Did you know that the largest demographic of readers are ? And Facebook is statistically their preferred venue used to learn about authors? For an author looking to reach the most people in one place, it's hard to do better. Thus, it is important to have your Facebook and other social media sites easily accessible from your author website and vice versa.

Although you do not have to post on social media every day, it is important that you remain active. There is so much activity and distractions online that it is *very* easy for visitors to lose interest. Take the time to learn how to automate posts. Facebook and Twitter both let you preschedule posts. This allows you to dedicate a block of time, say once every week, to create posts that might automatically appear every day. Learning how to do this, and being consistent with posting, helps you maintain your audience.

Also, unless you are writing about a controversial subject, be careful about how and what you post. Most readers are reading to accomplish one of two things. They either want to learn about something or to escape into a favorite topic or place. Try not to post anything that might unnecessarily drive potential readers away.

The single most important thing to remember about the Internet is creating your *brand*. Starting with your website, make your work *yours*. Then copy and promote your brand to your social media and to any site that is promoting your work, especially Amazon.com.

This part of your marketing experience can bring you a lot of pleasure as you interact with your reading public. Just make sure that the world is also getting to know about your work. After all, you may have written your book to make yourself happy, but we are sure that you also want as many people as possible to enjoy it, too.

FORMAT, LAYOUT & DESIGN

"How many pages should I write for my book?"

All book publishers and book designers have a standard they go by to estimate page length. Some go by pages; others go by words.

One rule of thumb is you can get 60 percent of a manuscript page into one typeset page (said manuscript being in 12-point type, double-spaced, preferably Times New Roman, with one-inch margins on an 8.5 × 11-inch document).

Another rule of thumb is you can get 250 to 300 words on a typeset page. This estimate will vary depending on the typeface, point size, and leading you use, as well as the trim size or physical size of the page—typically, it refers to a trade paperback, which is a 6 × 9-inch trim. So, a 55,000-word manuscript is about 220 typeset pages, and a 100,000-word manuscript is about 400 typeset pages.

Both rules of thumb are imperfect, but we've found the "250-300 word per page" rule works better more often than the "60 percent per page" rule.

How to Format Your Page

If you use the industry standard of 12-point type, double-spaced, Times New Roman, one-inch margins, 8.5 × 11 document, you'll make your editor and publisher happy, even in these days of modern technology. Formatting your page this way will help your publisher determine ending page count no matter how they estimate pages.

There are a few other industry standards you might note when formatting your manuscript pages.

Left-align your type and keep the right side ragged.

Single space after periods.

Indent paragraphs except for the opening paragraph of a chapter or section. (Set your indention in your paragraph formatting; don't use the tab key.)

Begin new chapters on new pages about one-third of the page down from the top. Center the title.

Use a word from the title (or a very shortened title) and your last name in the header, along with the page number.

Use italics for emphasis; never underline and never use bold italics (unless your heading is in bold).

If you prefer to use all caps for emphasis, remember that you're shouting—no one likes to be shouted at all the time. Your editor may change your all caps to italics. Maybe you should do that before your editor sees the manuscript?

Center the octothorp (#)—which you know as the hash sign, hashtag, number sign, or pound sign (it has several names that depend on context)—one blank line down from the end of your manuscript to signify the end of the document. You can also type "The End" if you like. Why? It's a holdover from printed manuscripts and screenplays to show there are no missing pages.

This isn't an industry standard, but it is helpful: If you know the publishing house's editorial style, use it, especially for items like book and movie titles, numbers, and references.

What's the Best Page Length for a Book?

There are no hard-and-fast rules for the number of pages in a book. There are, however, some guidelines.

Novels are often between 40,000 and 200,000 words. Subgenres vary. Children's books are 10,000 to 15,000. Mysteries and young adult books run between 40,000 and 80,000 words. Thrillers and epic fantasy often clock in at over 100,000 words.

The Science Fiction and Fantasy Writers of America offers a less nebulous guideline for the coveted Nebula award: a short story is under 7,500 words; a novella is 17,500 to 39,999 words; a novel is 40,000 words or over.

Nonfiction books also vary tremendously in word count. Short and punchy books are 40,000 to 60,000 words, but many nonfiction books are lengthy: 80,000 words and up.

In all cases, you can find an author who has successfully pushed the envelope one way or another. The best guideline you can follow is to make your book as long as it needs to be and no longer.

Book size (POD)

Print-on-demand (POD) technology has greatly improved in the past few years, and most POD printers are able to offer a number of book (or trim) sizes and bindings. Black-and-white books can have trim sizes ranging from 4″ x 6″ to 8 1/2″ x 11″ and print books between 14 to 1,050 pages. Color books have the same trims available and print books between eight and 250 pages.

The most common trim sizes for standard trade fiction and nonfiction books include: 5″ x 8″, 5.5″ x 8.5″, and 6″ x 9″. But there are a number of other trim size options you can choose from.

Trim Size

"Trim size" is essentially the publishing term for "book size." After each copy is printed and bound, the book is mechanically "trimmed" so that the size of every page is uniform. The trim size relates these dimensions, in Width x Height format.

In the U.S., the trim size is denoted in inches; in Europe, it's in millimeters.

Spine

The Spine of a book refers to the outside edge of the book where the pages are gathered and bound.

In addition to providing an anchor point for the pages, the spine provides the hinge action that allows the book's cover and pages to open and close.

Printing on the Spine

In most cases, the spines of hard cover books and perfect bound books are wide enough to be printed upon. However, the number of pages and the thickness of the pages are what determines the width of a book's spine. The wider the spine, the more surface area it provides for printed information. Printing the title and other features on a book's spine allows the book to be identified while it stands vertically on a shelf or lies horizontally in a stack.

What goes on which side of book?

Author name on left side

New chapters and sections should begin on the right side of an open book

Book title on right side

There are some widely-accepted practices that professionals use when creating the artwork layout for a printed book...

When it comes to adding page numbers to a book's content, there are few absolute rules.

1) Make sure odd and even page numbers are placed correctly.

When a book is opened, pages on the right hand side (known as recto) should always have an odd page number (1, 67, 213)...whereas pages on the left hand side (known as verso) should always have an even page number (2, 68, 214). Not adhering to this standard will have a negative impact on the appearance of the book.

2) Do not place page numbers near the inside margin.

You might be surprised how often we receive book artwork files that, if printed, would incorrectly place page numbers near the inside margin...making them very awkward to reference because they would print close to the book's spine. Always review your artwork file before submission to make sure all page numbers are properly placed. Page numbers should either appear near the outer margin of the page (in the lower or upper corner) or be centered at the bottom or top of the page.

3) There is no need to add numbers to blank pages.

It is common for there to be some blank pages within the main body of a book. Since new chapters and sections should begin on the right side of an open book, the page to the immediate left is sometimes blank. Even though these blank pages are included in the book's page numbering sequence, they do not need to receive a printed page number. For example, let's say page 40 is completely blank. The page before it would be numbered as page 39 and the page after it would be numbered as page 41. Page 40 still counts as a page, but it doesn't need a printed number.

4) Front matter should not be included in the book's main pagination.

Certain pages, such as the Copyright page, Dedication, Forward, Table of Contents, and so forth will appear before the book's core content. These pages should not be included in the book's main numbering sequence (1, 2, 3, 4, etc.). Instead, these pages are traditionally labeled with small Roman numerals (i, ii, iii, iv, etc.) or not numbered at all.

5) Don't put the page numbers too close to the edge of the paper.

Depending on the production method, the pages of your book may be printed on large sheets and then trimmed down to your desired page size. So, it is imperative to place the page numbers well inside the trim lines. Otherwise the numbers could end up too close to a trimmed edge, which will disrupt the aesthetics of the page layout. For best appearance, try to aim for a minimum distance of 1/4" from the edge of the page.

INTERIOR PARTS

Interior Parts of the books and their meaning

Title

For obvious reasons, your title is important...

But that is not all that's important to your book. The title page is also necessary and without it, your book will be missing something crucial.

Your title page serves as a means of not only declaring your title clearly, but also ensuring your name, subtitle, endorsement, and any other crucial information is present for your readers to view clearly.

Have you ever seen a book without a title? I doubt you did. Every book has their own title, they may not be unique, but they will have a title on their front page. A title signifies or is the main topic for a certain book. Example is when you read a book with a title of "Algebra", the first thing that you will think that it is a book of math algebra. It also identifies or it serves as a hint on what the book content is all about.

Author

Every book has their own author, they are the one who wrote the book. It is important to write the author for a book because this will signify that he was the one who wrote the book and that it was his idea. Once a book was plagiarized, the author can apply the copyright law for the one who copied the book.

Publisher

This is the company that prints the books.

Illustrator

This depends if the book has its image, some books don't have image so they won't need an illustrator. Basically, illustrators are the one who draw pictures for a book.

Copyright

Your book needs to be copyrighted. Unless you're okay with others stealing its content and reaping the rewards for themselves, that is.

We have a great guide on what it takes to copyright a book right here for you to view, but here are some of the basics.

Technically a book is copyrighted as you write it. But if you want it to be fully legal, you do have to pay to have it copyrighted.

Your copyright content will change depending on the type of book you're writing.

There are certain copyrights you cannot have exclusive rights to depending on what you cover in your book, which is usually impacted the most by what you write in a memoir and its legality

Acknowledgements

We all have people in our lives to acknowledge for our success in writing a book.

Much like the dedication, the acknowledgements are meant to recognize impactful people in our lives. These, unlike the dedication, typically come at the end of the book and can be written in longer, paragraph form as a pose to a short sentence for each.

Preface

This is an introduction of written by the author for a book. It usually has acknowledgement for those who assisted the author in his work.

Introduction

Most nonfiction books include an introduction to the book— a chapter before your first chapter as a means to introduce yourself and your credibility or author on the subject matter to your readers.

Your book introduction is extremely important for showing your readers why they should read the book and how you're the person to help them with whatever problem your book solves.

One of the best ways to do this is to first establish the pain-points your book helps to solve, and then make it clear how you, someone they don't know, can help with this issue.

This usually involves some of your own backstory, but keep it specific to the problem at hand. Your readers don't need an entire rundown of your personal history.

Prologue

What is a prologue?

A prologue is a short chapter that usually takes place before the main story begins as a means of granting understanding to the reader. It's also used to increase intrigue and captivate readers.

Not all books require prologues and in fact, if you can write your novel without it, that's actually preferred as many readers skip the prologue altogether.

Below is an example of a prologue from the very popular Game of Thrones by George R.R. Martin.

Dedication

A book dedication is a way for authors to bestow a high honor on a person (or small group of people) they want to praise or otherwise spotlight.

Table of Contents

This contains list of all the pages.

Text

This is where the content is put. They also call this as the body of the book. It contains all the information, story, etc. of a book.

Sections of a book

This will mostly pertain to nonfiction authors. We'll cover the fiction equivalent in the next section.

Some nonfiction books are written with different parts. These are usually separated into 3 parts that make up a greater whole in the book.

For example, in the book I'm currently writing, I break it up into 3 separate sections. Each part has its own focus and theme but they all work with one another to achieve a greater purpose.

Here's an example of how the sections of my book work:

Each part of this book has a main focus and theme, but when utilized together, they form a solution to a larger problem.

Epilogue

Not all book series get happily-ever-after endings. When your book series ends but you want a way to let the readers know what's in store for the characters' futures, an epilogue is a strong way to do that.

An epilogue is a short chapter that comes after the last chapter of a book as a way to tie the story together in a conclusion.

Essentially, the epilogue is the answer to the question, "what happens to them next?" This serves as a more satisfying way to let readers know that characters live "happily ever after."

Sometimes the ending of the story isn't satisfying enough for readers.

That part of their story may end, but if your readers want a more in-depth look at their life "after" the story, that's when an epilogue would come into play to tie everything together.

Appendix

This is an additional matter that the author writes at the end of the book. This can be a document, text, etc.

Glossary

This is commonly seen at the back end of the book. This is a list of words used by the author, usually industry words. The glossary often includes the definition of key words.

Index

This is like the glossary except that it lists the names, subjects, etc with reference to where they occur. This can also be found at the end of the book.

Bibliography

This is a list of the books of a specific author or publisher, or on a specific subject.

Author Bio

Not all books contain an author bio in it, specifically fiction (unless it's a hardback copy).

Nonfiction, however, is a type where the author bio can be at the bottom of the back page of your book, beneath the back cover synopsis.

Coming soon / Read more

This part of a book might not matter to you unless you have a book series or multiple books to your name.

The coming soon and read more pages are used to help your readers purchase and read more of your books.

This section of a book often comes at the very end, after your epilogue and acknowledgments. It's a single page with the cover images of your other book/s, their titles, and links for your ebook copy. This not only makes it easier for your readers to buy the next book, but it's also a great way to sell more books overall.

Back cover or synopsis of a book

I saved the best (and most important) for last. The back cover, also known as the synopsis of your book, is by far the most critical for getting people to buy.

Without a good synopsis to hook readers and buy them into your book, you won't sell.

These are crucial for both fiction and nonfiction.

With your fiction synopsis, you want to create intrigue and show your readers that they'll get a good story. The trick is doing this with a few short paragraphs.

As you can see, these look very different, though they serve the same purpose. The back of your book is the first thing someone reads in order to decide if they want to buy your book.

Make it concise, convincing, and show them the value they'll get from reading it—be that an entertaining read or a solution to their problem.

THE NEW PUBLISHING WORLD

The Publishing World Has Changed

Print On Demand

Save time and money

General Rule: Buy very few printed copies. Apply the savings to marketing.

The hardest lesson to learn when publishing your book is understanding that most publishers do not understand how the marketing of books has changed in just the last two years.

No longer is there only a choice between traditional publishing or vanity publishing. (Traditional publishing; where you receive a payment for your work, and vanity publishing; where you get your book printed so you can show it off to your friends and family.) Today, you can still go the traditional publishing route, assuming that you are either famous or infamous in some way. Or, you can take advantage of the world of self-publishing, where you can make far more money per book and determine your own destiny.

But the advancements in the self-publishing industry are not the only significant changes. We can thank Amazon.com for breaking the ice for self-publishers to be able to market their own work. And that's the key, learning how to *market* your work.

Unfortunately, most self-publishing companies are not much better than glorified printers. To avoid the pitfalls of choosing the wrong firm, you must learn what questions are important to ask before making your decision. But there is good news. More and more self-publishing companies are beginning to understand their own weaknesses. They are seeking out consultants or hiring the necessary people to handle the evolving industry.

Here's what has changed to make self-publishing the way to go for many authors.

First and foremost, there is no longer any need for an author to pre-purchase hundreds, even thousands of books, to get the best per-unit cost. Print-on-demand has completely revolutionized the industry. Plus, half the books purchased today are digital, requiring no printing at all. Companies, like Ingram Sparks and LuLu, understand this and can save you all kinds of money compared to the warehousing of your unnecessary inventory.

It does not stop there. The new tricks-of-the-trade that are understood by only a few consultants and publishers can almost magically take your book directly from the editor to becoming a bestseller overnight. It may seem like a simple concept, but just choosing the right colors for your cover and adding a sub-title to your book can make a huge difference. Does your potential publisher understand this and know what to do?

So, for all of you want-to-be authors who are considering the self-publishing route, please understand what questions you need to ask. And the first question is not, "How much is it going to cost to print my book?" Your primary concern should be, "How are you going to assist me with the marketing of my book?" And... "What do **I** have to do to market my book?"

The primary change in the publishing industry is where books are purchased: The Internet.

Sadly, in the next five years, if not sooner, the brick-and-mortar bookstores will probably become extinct. If the remaining chains are smart, they will partner with the big-box stores to take advantage of their customer traffic. With this in mind, the traditional distribution systems that concentrate on getting retailers to stock your books will go the way of the dinosaurs.

Understanding and taking advantage of this evolution is what most publishers, both traditional and independent, do not completely understand. Simply stated, the public is searching for their next read by typing keywords and topics into their mobile devices. Do you know how to make their searches result in your book popping up? Does your publisher know how to do this?

REBELL Books and Self Publisher Guide were founded because of the horror stories told by frustrated authors. A great example of this is told by one of the founder's experiences, Samuel Wardwell.

Back in 2015, Samuel Wardwell queried dozens of traditional publishers and agents about handling his new fictional novel, *Retribution*. He was turned down by every single one of them. The majority basically told him, "We don't know who you are." Because of this, Samuel chose to go the self-publishing route.

Like most authors, Samuel did a lot of research. He settled on a firm that was the self-publishing arm of a major traditional publishing house. They did a beautiful job editing his work, creating a cover, and formatting his book. The end product was wonderful, or so Samuel thought.

The next thing his publisher did was convince Samuel to purchase over 1000 copies of his book. This was to get the best per-unit-cost. Then, the distribution process started. Samuel thought he was on his way to success. After all, his story was great. It was well written. And he had the might of a well-known publishing house helping with the distribution of his book.

But it ended there. The books started to be returned from the retailers for lack of sales. Samuel ended up having to pay for these returns destroying any potential royalties for the few books that did sell. The next thing Samuel knew was everything ground to a halt. He now had a warehouse full of books with no way to sell them. His publisher had not prepared him for what was needed to market his work.

Samuel Wardwell did not give up there. He quickly realized that he was dealing with a glorified printing house. They had made their money by convincing him to pay for the printing of over a thousand books. Even though his book was only one of four completed, he received no help with his marketing.

That's when he sought out and found REBELL Books.

REBELL Books was not a publisher. They were a consulting firm. REBELL Books specialized in assisting authors with the proper preparation, set-up, and necessary marketing techniques to make a book successful.

As explained earlier, Samuel Wardwell's book was transformed by modifying its cover and adding a simple subtitle. Then, his website and social media were modified to promote not just Samuel's books but also himself, the author. These simple changes and the understanding of how people find their next read and how the book industry has so dramatically changed turned the tide for Samuel.

Samuel Wardwell's books are now a success. Because of this and his desire to help other authors with their work, Samuel joined REBELL Books and together created Self Publisher Guide.

Self-Publisher Guide helps authors prepare both authors and their books to make them successful. Self-Publisher Guide is also one of the only consulting firms that helps other self-publishing companies with their author's marketing and distribution needs.

The majority of their business is assisting frustrated authors, like Samuel Wardwell, with their existing work. However, they also promote their services for authors still in the writing stages or starting their journey into the publishing world.

Yes, the publishing world has changed. Whether you choose to use Self Publisher Guide to assist you with your work and publishing needs or just want to learn what is necessary to make sure you are not going to end up with hundreds of books with nowhere to sell them, let us be your guide.

The publishing industry has changed, in most ways for the better. Today, authors can choose their own destiny and drive their own success. 3000 new books are published and released every day! Ninety-nine percent of them end up gathering dust in a warehouse or decorating a frustrated author's bookshelf at home. There is a way to get your work out there and to make your book a success.

The key is understanding how your potential reader finds their next book and how to make your work what they see first. Like anything in life, understanding the rules and the tricks-of-thetrade is not cheating. It's smart, and the best way for you to obtain success and happiness with your work.

Distribution

You Must Have Global Book Distribution

When you plug into any of the large Global Book Distribution Networks you'll gain access to over 40,000

Independent bookstores – Online stores – Chain stores – Ebook retailers – Libraries – Universities – Retailers – Schools – E-commerce companies – Amazon – Barnes & Noble – Independent bookstores – Chapters / Indigo (Canada) – and other well-known book retailers and wholesalers across North America.

You'll also get RETAILERS , WHOLESALERS and BOOKCLUBS

You must get your book in front of buyers *Online, In Stores, and Around the World*

The Business of Publishing

Where do you begin?

Do not be afraid to seek professional advice. It's generally free and only takes a few hours of your time but can save your thousands of dollars!

There are several reputable advisors that will provide for you what traditional publishers do for their Authors. Advice on Design, Format, Publish, Distribute, Market and Promote Your Books.

If you are not sure who to talk to or what you really need, contact SELF PUBLISHER GUIDE we can offer valuable instruction from our panel of experts. We offer comprehensive book project evaluations. This preliminary overview of your book, idea or manuscript allows you to understand what it will take to make your book a success and what your next steps should entail.

The following are a few topics that you may want to seek professional assistance. They are generally affordable and easy to budget for.

Pre-Orders

Pre-orders are important! The most obvious reason would be bestseller lists. Pre-orders count toward first-week sales that often determine whether a book winds up on a bestselling list, Good first-week sales also land your book in the FEATURED BOOK category.

Ad Campaigns

We target Amazon, Google, and Social Media to publicize your work

Author Promotion

Set up book signings, appearances, public speaking, author and book promotions.

Website Integration

Tie all of your social media, blog, podcast and marketing platforms to your website.

Social Media Presence

Develop a following on Facebook, Twitter, Linkedin, Goodreads, and Patreon, etc

Keywords & Genre

Select the best keywords and genre-to make sure your book stands out during a search.

Cover Design

Learn the secret industry rules of color selection, fonts, subtitles, and layouts.

Blogging & Vlogging

Create an interesting blog and/or video log. It is important to be consistent with both.

Podcast

Create or share your podcasts economically. Learn how to provide easy access to your audience.

Book Launching

Launch or re-launch your book the right way. Promote and release your book as a bestseller.

Distribution

Get your book in front of buyers...Online, In Stores, book buyers & wholesalers. Amazon – Barnes & Noble

Directory & Lists

List your books with all of the book buyers & wholesalers. Amazon – Barnes & Noble – Independent bookstores, etc

Editing & Proofing

We offer both copy-editing and comprehensive editing for your work. Also free Book evaluations for existing books.

Frequently Asked Questions

Here are frequently asked questions. They are in no specific order, but should all be considered when writing your book.

What is the standard book size?

In general, you typically won't go wrong if you base your book size on a 6" x 9" format, which translates into **"for every inch of width, have one-and-a-half inches of height."** In today's world of books, over half of all new entries are read electronic devices. Although most technology can be set to read almost any book size, it is easier to set up the 6" x 9" format. Of course, some books are subject to their content and how you want to present your work. But in general, you are safe to use 6" x 9" or to use the formula mentioned above.

How many pages should be in a book?

This usually depends on what your genre is going to be. For instance, this book is solely geared toward supplying information and reference material for authors. On the other hand, a fictional novel can be as long as it takes to tell your story. In general, you want to take into account what your work is about, how it needs to be presented, and your target audience. Again, remember that most books are read in a digital format. So, you need to make sure that what you have created is easy to navigate and, unfortunately, easy to lay down. Today, even the best novel or self-help book must be designed for what we call "burst" reading. With this in mind, try to make each chapter or subject only a few pages long. This way, all readers can enjoy your work and not have to dedicate long blocks of time to your book. This is especially important when writing works of fiction. Always try to keep your chapters down to just a few pages. This way, even a large book can be absorbed the same way one eats an elephant... One bite at a time.

How many words are too many in a book?

This question is asked mostly by writers of fiction. Most publishers get concerned when a book is more than 150,000 words.

When deciding the length of a book, you must always take into account your reading audience. Based on a 6" x 9" format and using a size 12 font, a 150K-word novel is about 400 to 425 pages. If this is a hardcover book, then anything longer can become unwieldy. When getting past 150K word count, start to consider whether your book might be better presented in multiple parts. (E.g. "Part 1," Part 2," etc.) Most works of fiction or even non-fiction usually have between an 80K and 120K word count.

However, do not let this deter you. Just keep in mind that a long book is very rarely read in one sitting. Always make sure that your chapters are relatively short. And try to make it easy for your reader to lay down your book and to be able to quickly continue it later when time allows.

Which page is "page one" in a book?

Most publishers prefer to format "page one" (or where the actual number on the bottom of the page is "1") when the primary story or subject actually begins. Things like the publisher's information page, dedication page, table of contents, and even the prologue usually either have no page numbers or use Roman numerals counting down backward to the actual beginning of the book/story. The reason for this is to make it easier to set up your table of contents. It also gives your reader a better idea of how long your book actually is.

What is the best font-theme and font-size?

There has been a hot and ongoing debate over which font-theme to use. "Times New Roman" is still considered the industry standard. Historically, this is because almost all typewriters were manufactured this way. Most publishers prefer that your manuscript be submitted doublespaced, using a 12 pts font-size, and in "Times New Roman."

Realistically, none of this really matters anymore, since it is so easy to change font theme, size, and spacing.

But one thing to keep in mind is your reader's ease-of-reading. Any font size smaller than 12 pts can make it difficult to read your work. In general, we are all used to reading "Times New Roman." So, if you are going to go outside of industry norm, you really want to have a good reason for doing so.

What side of a page does a chapter begin?

It is not unusual to end up with a lot of blank pages in a completed book. This is because most chapters begin on the front of a page, rather than the back. It is also common for this new chapter-info-page to only have the chapter-number and title with a blank page opposite to it. This means that the actual info/story always starts on the back of the chapter-info page. Writers should take all of these incidental blank pages into account when determining the size of their book.

Hardcover vs. Paperback?

Hardcover books typically have a greater lifespan and are more durable. For the most part, the cover design can be duplicated and lose almost none of its design features in either hardcover or paperback format. The real determining factor is cost. The larger the book, the more expensive a hardcover is going to be, while a softcover book is far cheaper and easier to handle.

When we think of paperback books, especially novels, we mistakenly think of a second printing or a discounted version of the original hardback version. This is becoming less and less true today. Many novels are printed with a softcover to reduce the wholesale price to book aggregators and distributors. If you are a new/unknown author with a work of fiction or non-fiction, you might want to consider the paperback format initially. Your per-book costs and shipping fees end up being dramatically reduced. The book is also much easier to hold and read.

Self-help and information books almost always are better in hardcover. Again, it depends upon their size. Also, if your book contains a lot of pictures or diagrams, a hardcover will protect them better and be more durable.

Self-publishing vs. Conventional Publishing?

There are techniques that can be used to get your foot in the door of a conventional publishing firm. However, the key to doing this is convincing them that you have a preexisting market that is interested in your work. Your challenge... Having a preexisting market for your books. This is especially true for authors of fiction/non-fiction works.

Most of us have no choice but to self-publish. For the most part, if you are not famous or infamous, a conventional publisher will not even give you the time of day. This is true for agents, too.

Over the last few years, the entire publishing industry has gone through a monumental change. Most publishing companies, both conventional or otherwise, have not kept up. Publishing a book and using traditional distribution methods no longer works for most authors. With this in mind, almost without exception, you are better off self-publishing.

But, you must understand that you *now* are your own publisher! This concept is very important to understand.

Most self-publishing firms are really just overblown printing companies. They do a great job creating a pretty cover, editing and formatting your book, and then handing you a real live copy of your masterpiece... After convincing you to purchase hundreds of copies or your own work. What they do not understand or prepare you for is the marketing side of the business. How do you find an audience for your book?

On the other hand, you are able to make far more money on each book sold by going the self-publishing route. What you need to do is make sure you ask the right questions of your publisher-to-be and to be prepared for the marketing and social media requirements to make your work a success.

If you are already famous or have a few thousand friends interested in your work, then you certainly can go the traditional route. They'll be happy to publish your work. But if you are unknown, believe that you have a great product, and are willing to put the time and dedication into your marketing, then you are far better off going the self-publishing route.

The trick... Make sure you know what questions to ask your publisher-to-be and, if you can, start creating your social media presence **as** you are writing your book rather than waiting until you are done.

Do I need to get copies of the cover-proofs and the formatted book?

The answer to this question is yes, absolutely, always, and "Make sure you do!"

Seriously, your work is your property. Do not let your publisher tell you anything different. Always make sure that when you sign a publishing contract that you have the exclusive rights to your work and anything created during the process of editing, formatting, and the designing of the artwork, especially the cover.

It is very common for authors to change publishers. This is especially true in the self publishing world. Consider this... If your book is a great success, then you will become inherently famous. You might choose to sign with a literary agent or a traditional publishing house. On the other hand, if your publisher screws up or you choose to change firms, you want to have all of your work safely stored and under your control.

Always make sure you have the digital files of all of your book's components.

When typing my work, is there anything I should worry about?

If you want to drive your editor nuts, then overuse your return/enter button on your keyboard.

Many of us learned to type on a typewriter or using a basic word processing program. It never occurred to us that every time we hit the enter button that we were creating an obstacle for our editors to hurdle.

The picture below is taken from the top of Microsoft Word's toolbar. When you open Word, click on "Home," then look for the section marked "Paragraph." Now, click on the ¶. (It is located in the upper right corner, as shown below.) You will be amazed at how many times you have used your "Enter" button.

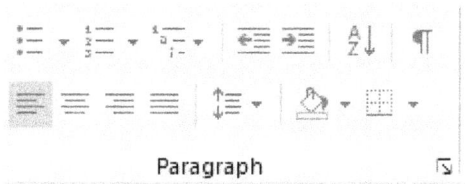

Paragraph

What you will see in your Word document (this is true with most word processing programs), are a series of ¶ symbols plastered all over your work. If you want to save your editor or yourself, if you are doing your own formatting, a lot of time, *do not use the "Enter" key when moving from one chapter to another.* Also, just as important, if you want to have a picture or diagram located on its own page, do not use the "Enter" key to move to that new location.

What you want to do is use the "Page Break" button. For example, this option is located in the "Insert" field on your Microsoft Word toolbar, as shown in the diagram below. Just choose "Insert" and then click on "Page Break." This feature should be used every time you need a new page for chapters, pictures, or diagrams.

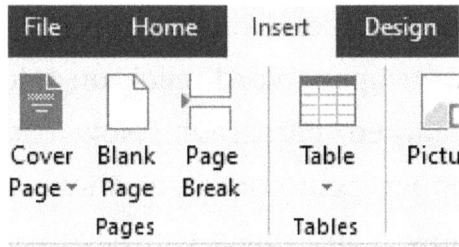

By using "Page Break" and being cognizant of your use of the "Enter" key, you will make the editing and formatting process much easier. All word processing software has a "Page Break" feature. If you are not using Microsoft Word, then learn where the "Page Break" feature is located and use it.

What defines a bestseller?

First, let's talk about what it means to be a "Bestseller."

In short, the term bestseller means different things to different people and entities. For instance, most New York Time's bestselling books typically sell at least 5000 copies in a span of one week.

But you can still become a bestselling author and not necessarily garner a mention in a major publication. As an author, your goal is to be able to use the moniker of "Bestselling" author. If you have properly interviewed your publisher and discovered if their marketing people understand what is required, almost any book can be a "Bestseller." Remember, you want to be able to use the designation. The trick is in understanding how to become a bestselling author in your category. Unless you just want your book to sit on your own coffee table, make sure you are working with a publishing firm who knows what is needed to allow you to use the designation.

Many authors are surprised to learn that it only takes 5000 copies sold of any book to be considered a *success* in the publishing world. You might also be intrigued to learn that with the right marketing, almost any book can be a success and make your work profitable.

Do I need an editor?

After all, you do use editing software... right?

Have you ever read a book that is poorly edited? *Do not* make the mistake of making your book one of those. You can have the most beautiful cover work and the greatest marketing approach ever. But if your book is not edited by a professional, it's going to come back to haunt you big time.

The challenge is understanding that you *cannot* edit your own work. Editing software, like Grammarly, is great for making sure that your punctuation and spelling are correct. Good software is even able to pick up poor sentence structure and misuse of the English language (which is really, really easy to do). However, you also need a trained eye to take a look at your content. This is especially true if you are writing fiction/non-fiction works. What you see in your own mind does not always translate to the written page smoothly, and your reader may misunderstand your motivation and intent.

Editors typically charge between 2 to 5 cents per word for their services. Believe me when I say, "It is worth it." A poorly edited book is not only difficult to read, but it can also lead to it never being finished.

Another challenge in the editing world is to make sure that your self-help or how-to books are understandable to everyone. Simple things like transposing words or not following up later in your book about an important topic or subject can make it difficult for your reader to understand your work.

A great example of a lack of editing is when your work is translated into another language. Have you ever wondered why Ikea uses very few words in their assembly instructions? They learned the hard way that when something is translated from Swedish to Chinese, then into English that words can be totally lost or poorly substituted.

Always have a trained eye review your work.

When to use i.e. or E.g.

While similar, they are not interchangeable.

I.e. stands for id, est, or 'that is' -- and it's used to clarify a statement or word that came before it.

E.g. means *exempli gratia* or "for example." It's used to introduce examples and illustrate a statement.

Please feel free to ask us additional questions.

If your question can help our readers, we may add them to future additions of this book. Just go to our contact page located at the end or email questions to:

info@RebellBooks.com

Real Life Rejections to Success

The Tale of Peter Rabbit by Beatrix Potter was rejected so many times she decided to self-publish 250 copies. It has now sold 45 million copies.

After 5 years of continual rejection, the writer finally lands a publishing deal: Agatha Christie. Her book sales are now in excess of $2 billion. Only William Shakespeare has sold more.

The Christopher Little Literary Agency received 12 publishing rejections in a row for their new client, until the eight-year-old daughter of a Bloomsbury editor demands to read the rest of the book. The editor agrees to publish but advises the writer to get a day job since she has little chance of making money in children's books. Yet *Harry Potter and the Philosopher's Stone* by J.K. Rowling spawned a series where the last four novels consecutively set records as the fastest-selling books in history, on both sides of the Atlantic, with combined sales of $450 million.

Louis L'Amour received 200 rejections before Bantam took a chance on him. He is now their best-ever selling author with $330 million sales.

"Too different from other juveniles on the market to warrant its selling."A rejection letter sent to <u>Dr Seuss.</u> $300 million sales and the 9th best-selling fiction author of all time.

"You have no business being a writer and should give up." <u>Zane Grey</u> ignored the advice. There are believed to be over 250 million copies of his books in print.

140 rejections stating **"Anthologies don't sell"** until the *<u>Chicken Soup for the Soul</u>* series by <u>Jack Canfield & Mark Victor Hansen</u> sells 125 million copies.

The years of rejection do not break his spirit. He only becomes more determined to succeed. When he eventually lands a publishing deal, such is the demand for his fiction that it is translated into over 47 languages, as **The Chronicles of Narnia** by <u>C.S. Lewis</u> goes on to sell over 100 million copies.

"It is so badly written." The author tries <u>Doubleday</u> instead and his little book makes an impression. **The Da Vinci Code**, by Dan Brown, sells 80 million copies.

After two years of rejections stating that her fiction would have no readership, <u>Reilly and Lee</u> agree to publish **The One in the Middle Is the Green Kangaroo**, launching the career of the best-selling author <u>Judy Blume.</u> Combined sales: 80 million copies.

Having sold only 800 copies on its limited first release, the author finds a new publisher and **The Alchemist** by <u>Paulo Coelho</u> sells 75 million copies.

"We feel that we don't know the central character well enough." The author does a rewrite and his protagonist becomes an icon for a generation as **The Catcher In The Rye** by <u>J.D. Salinger</u> sells 65 million copies.

5 publishers reject <u>L.M. Montgomery</u>'s debut novel. Two years after this rejection, she removes it from a hat box and resubmits. L.C. Page & Company agrees to publish **Anne of Green Gables** and it goes on to sell 50 million copies.

"I recommend that it be buried under a stone for a thousand years." Shunned by all the major publishers, the author goes to France and lands a deal with <u>Olympia Press.</u> The first 5000 copies quickly sell out. But the author <u>Vladimir Nabokov</u> now sees his novel, **Lolita**, published by all those that initially turned it down, with combined sales of 50 million copies.

The Tale of Peter Rabbit by <u>Beatrix Potter</u> was rejected so many times she decided to self-publish 250 copies. It has now sold over 45 million.

"*Nobody will want to read a book about a seagull.*" Richard Bach's *Jonathan Livingston Seagull* goes on to sell 44 million copies.

"*Undisciplined, rambling and thoroughly amateurish writer.*" But Jacqueline Susann refuses to give up and her book the *Valley of the Dolls.* It sells 30 million copies.

Margaret Mitchell gets 38 rejections from publishers before finding one to publish her novel **Gone With The Wind**. It sells 30 million copies.

"*The girl doesn't, it seems to me, have a special perception or feeling which would lift that book above the 'curiosity' level.*" Perhaps the most misguided literary critique in history. With a further 15 rejections, there remained little hope that her personal thoughts would see the light of day. Eventually, Doubleday brings the translation to the world, and *The Diary of Anne Frank* sells 25 million copies.

"*A long, dull novel about an artist.*" Publisher rejects **Lust For Life** by Irving Stone. Yet, with persistence, he finds another publisher and sells 25 million copies.

"*An irresponsible holiday story that will never sell.*" Rejection of **The Wind In The Willows** by Kenneth Grahame. The novel did sell: 25 million copies worldwide.

His publishers **Doubleday** rejected the first 100 pages. So the author **Peter Benchley** starts from scratch and *Jaws* sells 20 million copies.

Thor Heyerdahl believes his book **Kon-Tiki: Across The Pacific** is unique. 20 publishers disagree. The 21st takes it on and sells 20 million: one-million copies for each rejection.

Despite 14 consecutive agency rejections **Stephenie Meyer**'s *Twilight* goes on to sell 17 million copies and spends 91 weeks on the New York Times best-seller list.

"An absurd and uninteresting fantasy which was rubbish and dull." Rejection letter sent to **William Golding** for **The Lord Of The Flies**. 15 million copies sold.

After 20 rejection letters, **WM Paul Young** self-publishes his novel **The Shack**. 15 million in sales and a cultural phenomenon.

Three years of rejection letters are kept in a bag under her bed. The bag becomes so heavy that she is unable to lift it. But **Meg Cabot** does not dwell on the failure. Instead she keeps sending her manuscript out. It gets taken on, and **The Princess Diaries** sells 15 million copies.

"**Too radical of a departure from traditional juvenile literature.**" L. Frank Baum persists and **The Wonderful Wizard Of Oz** sells 15 million copies.

Little, Brown & Company **passes on a two book deal for** Alice Walker. *When complete, she found another publisher for her her novel* **The Color Purple.** It sells 10 million copies and wins The Pulitzer Prize.

26 publishers reject **A Wrinkle in Time**. It wins the 1963 Newbery Medal and becomes an international best-seller. 8 million copies sold and counting.

"**Unsaleable and unpublishable.**" Publisher on Ayn Rand's **The Fountainhead**. Random House takes a chance on it. It sells 7 million copies in the US alone.

After 25 literary agents reject her debut manuscript, she mails it unsolicited to a small publisher in San Francisco, MacAdam/Cage. They believe it is a classic. Upon publication, the world agrees.

Translated into over 33 languages and adapted into a movie, **The Time Traveler's Wife** by Audrey Niffenegger sells 7 million copies.

To deal with publisher rejections, Hugh Prather decides to write a book about them in his early struggles and **Notes To Myself** sells 5 million copies.

To prove how hard it is for new writers to break in, Jerzy Kosinski uses a penname to submit his bestseller **Steps** to 13 literary agents and 14 publishers. All of them reject it, including Random House, who later decided to publish it.

"It was rejected 60 times. But letter number 61 was the one that accepted me. Three weeks later we sold the book to Amy Einhorn Books." Kathryn Stockett on the worldwide bestseller: **The Help**.

Rejected by publishers, Ruth Saberton leaves her 400 page manuscript **Katy Carter Wants a Hero** on the holiday home doormat of Richard and Judy in Cornwall. They love the book so much that their recommendation secures a publishing deal with Orion.

"Frenetic and scrambled prose." Viking Press disagrees, and publishes one of the most influential novels of all time. Since 1957, it has regularly sold at least 60,000 copies every year. **On The Road** by Jack Kerouac became a multi-million copy best-seller.

5 London publishers turn it down. The little book finally finds a home: **Life of Pi** by <u>Yann Martel,</u> won <u>The Man Booker Prize</u> in 2002.

100 literary agents and publishers reject it. <u>Andersen Press</u> does not and **Out of Shadows** by <u>Jason Wallace</u> wins the <u>Costa Children's Book Award.</u>

Rejected by 20 literary agents and publishers, one editor believes in the book and <u>Catherine O'Flynn</u>'s **What Was Lost** wins the 2008 <u>Costa Book Award.</u>

Rejected by his agent because it is narrated by a dog, <u>Garth Stein</u> switches to <u>Folio Literary Management</u> and **The Art Of Racing In The Rain** sells for 7 figures.

"An endless nightmare. I think the verdict would be 'Oh don't read that horrid book." Publisher rejects **The War Of The Worlds** by <u>H.G. Wells.</u> It is soon published in 1898, and has been in print ever since.

"Our united opinion is entirely against the book. It is very long, and rather oldfashioned." Publisher rejects **Moby Dick** by <u>Herman Melville.</u> It is later published by <u>Harper & Brothers,</u> who releases a first print run of 3000 copies. Only 50 of these sell during the author's lifetime. Today, it is in the top 100 most read books in history.

After 22 rejections, **Dubliners** is finally published. But it only sells 379 copies in the first year. James Joyce bought 120 of them.

T.S. Eliot as head of Faber & Faber rejects it because of **"Trotskyite politics."** Secker & Warburg spot potential, and George Orwell's **Animal Farm** becomes a best-seller.

"An absurd story as romance, melodrama or record of New York high life." Yet its publication sees **The Great Gatsby** by F.Scott Fitzgerald become a best-selling classic.

"Stick to teaching." Louisa May Alcott refuses to give up on her dream. **Little Women** sells millions, and is still in print 140 years later. Unlike the name of the publisher who told her to give up.

Rejected by leading publishers, the 21-year-old finally persuades a small publishing company Lackington, Hughes, Harding, Mavor, & Jones, to take a chance on her debut. They agree, but do not put her name on the cover, and only print 500 copies in 1818. Booksellers only bought 25 of them. Despite a named credit in 1822, sales did not improve, until a 3rd edition was published by Henry Colburn & Richard Bentley in 1831. Word of mouth combined with some of the finest prose ever written in the genre, quickly sees **Frankenstein** by Mary Shelley become a best-seller.

"I haven't the foggiest idea about what the man is trying to say. Apparently the author intends it to be funny." Publisher rejects **Catch-22** by Joseph Heller, a novel believed to have been given its name because it was the 22nd publisher, Simon and Schuster, who agreed to take it on. To date: 10 million copies sold.

"Older children will not like it because its language is too difficult." On **Watership Down** by Richard Adams, one of the fastest-selling books in history.

After Random House rejects his debut novel **The Long Walk** the author puts it away and ponders his next move. He decides to write a new novel: Stephen King tries again and creates **Carrie**. It is published by **Doubleday**.

Random House rejects **Carrie, "We are not interested in science fiction which deals with negative utopias. They do not sell."** Stephen King's chooses to change publishers. **Carrie** sells 1 million copies in the first year alone.

"The American public is not interested in China." Pearl S Buck's **The Good Earth** becomes the best-selling US novel two years running in 1931/32, and wins The Pulitzer Prize in the process.

With 23 rejections, Frank Herbert finally lands a publisher, and *Dune* becomes the best-selling science-fiction novel of all time.

24 literary agencies turned down **The Notebook** by Nicholas Sparks. The 25th did not and sold it to Time Warner one week later for $1 million dollars.

31 publishers in a row turn down **The Thomas Berryman Number**. It wins the Edgar for Best Novel becoming a best-seller for James Patterson. An author with 19 consecutive number #1's on the New York Times best-seller list and sales of 220 million.

16 literary agencies and 12 publishers reject **A Time To Kill**. Its modest print run of 5000 quickly sells out, as it goes on to become a best-seller for its author: John Grisham. Combined sales of 250 million.

Despite 17 rejections Patrick Dennis in 1956 becomes the first author in history to have 3 books ranked on the New York Times best-seller list at the same time. He had worked through publishers in alphabetical order. The one that finally agreed to take him on: Vanguard Press.

"It's Poland and the rich Jews again." Editor at Alfred A. Knopf publishing house rejects Isaac Singer. His book **Satan**

in Goray becomes a best-seller, and the author himself later wins the Nobel Prize for Literature in 1978.

30 publishers tell Laurence Peter that his book **The Peter Principle** will never sell. In 1969, a mere 18 months later it is a number #1 best-seller.

"This will set publishing back 25 years." Rejecting **The Deer Park**. Its author Norman Mailer goes on to win The Pulitzer Prize, twice.

Alex Haley writes for eight years and receives 200 consecutive rejections. His novel **Roots** becomes a publishing sensation, selling 1.5 million copies in its first seven months of release, and going on to sell 8 million. Such is the success that The Pulitzer Prize award the novel a Special Citation in 1977.

Taking on the advice of his 76 rejections Jasper Fforde writes a new book **The Eyre Affair** and it becomes an instant New York Times best-seller.

"Every last publisher in England rejected my first two books." So Simon Kernick writes a third and **The Business Of Dying** lands him a publishing deal with Bantam.

"*Utterly untranslatable.*" Jorge Luis Borges tries a different publisher. He wins 50 Literary Prizes and dies with his books in many languages.

"We suggest you get rid of all that Indian stuff." Publisher to Tony Hillerman, on his bestselling **Navajo Tribal Police** mystery novels.

Rejected by all publishers in the UK and US, the author self-publishes his novel in Florence, Italy, using his own press in 1928. After being banned for nearly 30 years, Grove Press publish the controversial work in 1959. A year later Penguin finally launch the UK edition. The book quickly sells millions, as **Lady Chatterly's Lover** by D.H. Lawrence becomes a worldwide best-seller.

Rejected by several publishers Jonathan Littell's **Les Bienveillantes** becomes the number #1 bestseller in France and wins The Goncourt Literary Prize.

Her literary agent believes in her. The publishers of New York do not. So Emily Giffin flies to London to write **Something Borrowed** and it goes on to become a New York Times best-seller.

Jacqueline Kennedy Onassis as an editor at Doubleday sees potential in Dorothy West's unfinished novel **The Wedding** and it later becomes a best-seller.

"Rejection slips could wallpaper my room." <u>Dennis Kimbro</u> on **Think and Grow Rich: A Black Choice** used now in seminars throughout the US.

Despite initial rejections, <u>E.C. Osondu</u> persists with his book **Waiting** and it wins the 2009 African Booker.

Rejected by everyone except Heinemann. <u>Chinua Achebe</u>'s **Things Fall Apart** becomes the most widely-read book in modern African literature.

"I rack my brains why a chap should need thirty pages to describe how he turns over in bed before going to sleep." French editor rejects **Remembrance of Things Pasts** by <u>Marcel Proust.</u> Now regarded as a literary classic, its word count would be a challenge for any editor: 1.5 million – making it the longest novel in the history of literature.

"We found the heroine boring." <u>Mary Higgins Clark</u> switches genre to suspense and her second book gets a $1.5 million advance. She is now on a $60 million book deal.

"This author is beyond psychiatric help. Do not publish." Publisher rejects **Crash** by <u>J.G. Ballard.</u> The author immediately declares this as sign of **"complete artistic success."** The novel goes on to inspire countless songs, and the film adaptation wins the <u>Jury Prize</u> at the <u>Cannes Film Festival</u> in 1996.

The **Alfred A. Knopf** publishing house turned down: **Jack Kerouac, George Orwell, Sylvia Plath,** and **Mario Puzo**'s **The Godfather**.

The **E.E. Cummings** best-seller **The Enormous Room** has a dedication page **'With No Thanks To'** all 15 publishers who turned it down.

"He hasn't got any future." Yet, publication of **The Spy Who Came in From the Cold** leads to its author, **John le Carré,** having one of the most distinguished careers in literary history.

Robert M. Pirsig's **Zen & the Art of Motorcycle Maintenance** is in the **Guinness Book Of Records** for 121 rejections, more than any other best-seller.

"Hopelessly bogged down and unreadable." The 1968 letter from an editor did not deter the author, **Ursula K. Le Guin,** as her book **The Left Hand of Darkness** goes on to become just the first of her many best-sellers, and is now regularly voted as the second best fantasy novel of all time, next to *The Lord of the Rings*.

After 21 rejections, Richard Hornberger switches to the pseudonym, **Richard Hooker,** and his debut novel becomes a phenomenal publishing success, spawning an **Oscar-**

Winning Film Adaptation, and one of the most watched Television shows in history: **M*A*S*H**.

"Good God, I can't publish this." So it finds itself at the offices of publishers Jonathan Cape and Harrison Smith instead, who immediately spots the talent of its author, and in 1931 propels him and his controversial, **Sanctuary**, into the literary limelight. The author, William Faulkner, goes on to become one of the most critically praised novelists of all time.

The estate of best-seller Jack London in San Francisco, the _House Of Happy Walls_ has a collection of some of the 600 rejections he received before selling a single story.

Glossary

Author Bio: Most readers want to know not only what your book is about but also who wrote it and why. You should create two author-bios. The first version goes on the back cover of your book and should be concise and to the point. A more in-depth version needs to be used for your website and Amazon.com author-page. Both versions should relate who you are and your motivation for creating your book.

Author Website: Your author website is your central hub for the distribution of your work. Everything from your social media to your listings on Amazon.com and other book retailers should direct your readers to your website. From there, you can take control and direct potential buyers. The site should promote your work and just as important be designed to capture their contact info for future marketing and networking.

Book Evaluations: This is the first step in your journey into making your book a published reality. If a publisher does not offer a book evaluation process, be suspicious that they are only a glorified printer and not interested in your marketing needs. Your book evaluator will first take a look at your synopsis (see "Book Synopsis" below) of your work, then read the first few chapters to determine what is needed to meet industry standards (see "Industry Standards" below). This is not a criticism or review of your work. The evaluation is to make sure that your book is ready to go through the editing and formatting process.

Book Synopsis: Like your author bio, you should create two versions of your book's synopsis. First, what is a synopsis? A synopsis is a brief description of something. In this case, your synopsis describes your book and what it entails. You want to create a short version for the back of your book cover and social media sites. A longer version that goes into more detail should be placed on your author website and any author-pages set up by your book distributors, like on Amazon.com.

Category & Genre: Genre is the type of book you have written. Category, or sub-category, defines the book's subject matter to help the reader find your work. Understanding your category and genre are important for the marketing side of your work. The most difficult genre to market is "fiction," because there is so much competition for the available reader's time. Your genre is set by industry standards, while your category and sub-category can be appropriately selected to assist search engines with assisting a reader with finding your book.

Copyright: A copyright allows you to register your book and lay a proprietary claim to its contents. This is especially important when working with exclusive information. A book's contents can be copyrighted, but the book's title cannot.

Direct-to-Reader: Direct-to-reader distribution systems are the most profitable for the author. This means that you are cutting out the retailer and selling your book directly from your publisher. Setting up your social media and even your author page on a retailer's websites can help direct buyers to your website where they can purchase your work "direct-to-reader" rather than from the retailer. Of course, you still want your readers to be able to use retailers to purchase your work. But it's always a plus if you can sell your book directly. Direct-to-reader purchases also allow you to capture your reader's contact information for future marketing.

Editor/Editing: There is a huge difference between editing and an "editor." First, always remember that it is almost impossible to edit your own work. As an author, you are too close to your own work. It is very easy to overlook things that are easily detected by an independent eye. Editing software is great as a first step. But always seek out a qualified editor to check for content, continuity, and those typing gaffs missed by your software. It's worth it in the long run.

Genre & Category: See "Category and Genre."

Glossary: A glossary, also known as an alphabetical list of terms in a particular domain of knowledge with the definitions for those terms. Traditionally, a glossary appears at the end of a book and includes terms within that book that are either newly introduced, uncommon, or specialized.

Industry Standards: When referring to industry standards, we are talking about known things that are either necessary to create a book or are known to make a book more successful. Things like the appropriate colors to use on the cover of your book to the placement of information both inside and on your book's cover are all a part of this. It is important that your publisher understands the industry standards for your book's genre and your distribution needs.

ISBN Code: The ISBN code is the barcode located on the back of our book. Within the code are your book's title, your name, and the list price (See "Price Determination" below) of the book. Also, permanently embedded in the code is where the item is manufactured. It is important that you make sure that your publisher knows what *kind* of an ISBN number your book is receiving. Most self-publishing companies do not realize that the ISBN code they are selling you allows retailers and distributors to know that your book is "self-published." This can be a turnoff for many aggregators and distributors in the industry. Done properly, your book's ISBN code can help with your work's distribution. Make sure that your publisher knows the difference.

Library of Congress Registration: Having an LCR for your book, even if it's not accepted into the Library of Congress's regular collection, is still important. As a unique identification number, it holds a place for book processing by libraries, book vendors, and the Library of Congress.

Price Determination: Do your homework before determining the list price of your book. Check out the retail price for other books in your genre and category. Take into account its size and whether it is hard or soft covered. The price will be embedded in your ISBN code and cannot be changed without re-publishing and changing the code. Books rarely sell for their list price. But they typically do *not* sell for *more* than the list price. You can always reduce the price of your book when promoting sales or offering a digital version.

Print-on-Demand: Print-on-demand is the way to go for most self-publishers. This allows you to *not* have to maintain an inventory and warehouse your books. Companies, like Amazon.com and LuLu, will print and ship your books as they are ordered. The quality is not reduced and will save you additional shipping and storage costs.

Royalties: Royalties are the monies distributed to the author after all expenses are calculated. It is important to understand when you are eligible to receive royalties. Because of how complicated the sales and distribution systems work in the publishing industry; royalties are typically paid out quarterly and then have to total a predetermined minimum to generate a check.

SSL Certificate: The Internet is evolving. One of the major changes is the need for an SSL

Certificate. SSL is short for "Secure Socket Layer." They are now required if you want your website to be secure. Without the SSL, most Internet security software will not allow you to enter the website without warning you. This could potentially scare off your visitors. SSL Certificates are small data files that digitally bind a cryptographic key to an organization's details. When installed on a web server, it activates the padlock and the https protocol and allows secure connections from a web server to a browser, a domain name, server name, or hostname. Typically, they have to be renewed annually.

Sub-Title: Almost without exception, your book should have a subtitle. A subtitle helps to make your book more unique.

The keywords used in your book placement for Internet searches should be based on your title and subtitle. By having a subtitle, your book will be easier to find.

Third-Party Endorsements: These endorsements are when you have either a relevant person or business put their credibility behind your work. When used correctly, they can be very helpful with the decision-making process of your potential readers. Keep in mind that *good* book reviews are preferable in the long run to the success of your book. But when first introducing your work to the public, a third-party endorsement can be helpful.

Self Publisher Guide

www.SelfPublisherGuide.com

Authors

Our publishing programs are designed to educate authors with everything necessary to promote both you and your work. It doesn't matter whether your book is fiction or non-fiction. We will show you just what is needed to get your hard work out to the reading public.

FREE CONSULTATION

www.ingramcontent.com/pod-product-compliance
Lightning Source LLC
Chambersburg PA
CBHW060444040426
42331CB00044B/2602